ΔLL OF IT IS YOU.

ΛLL OF IT IS YOU.

poetry

NICO TORTORELLΛ

CROWN
ARCHETYPE
NEW YORK

Crown Archetype and colophon is a registered trademark
of Penguin Random House LLC.

Library of Congress Cataloging-in-Publication Data is
available upon request.

ISBN 978-0-525-57653-2
Ebook ISBN 978-0-525-57654-9

Printed in the United States of America

Cover design by Michael Morris
Cover images: (hand) courtesy of the author;
(Da Vinci's *Vitruvian Man*) siart/Shutterstock; (stars)
Haitong Yu/Moment/Getty Images; (map) duncan 1890/
DigitalVision Vectors/Getty Images

10 9 8 7 6 5 4 3 2 1

First Edition

for you.

Contents

ALL OF IT IS YOU.

introduction.

all of it is you.
yes you,
my dear,
are all of it.

let it be said: this book has one of the greatest
titles of all time. when i came up with it, i imme-
diately went on a wild internet chase to see who or
where i would be adopting this inclusive, keenly inti-
mate mantra, and to my surprise, no one had used it.
until now.
all of it is you is the you in everything.
this book is the realest work i've ever created.
it represents more of me than anything i've put out
into the world. what i'm not going to say is that this
is the greatest collection of poetry ever written. i
would like to think i know where i stand in the lot
of legends that came before me, and the genius that
walk among. i also know that creating "perfection"
was never my goal. what makes a good poem? what makes
a poet great? is it in the intelligence, intellect
or intuition? is it in how well they can pack fancy
words together to create mind bending syntax? how well
they can use metaphor and allegory to paint even the
simplest of pictures? is it in the beatnik typewriter
font? does a poem have to be perfect? does the poet?
i'll be the first one to say i am not an expert on
anything at all. in fact, quite the opposite. to let
you in on a little secret, my greatest insecurity has
always been my own intelligence. am i smart enough?
and even if so, will people care given the shell that
holds it? i have exposed myself physically and emo-
tionally in more ways than most people do in a life-
time, but i've never really let the world hold my own
complex inner workings quite like this. and let me
tell you, i feel very exposed.

the goal for this book, and every day for myself, is to be a physical manifestation of process and journey. i strive to live my life in an unconditionally raw, loving, engaging, curious way, and that's exactly how i approached writing. i probed at the subjects, ideas and theories that rile me up on the human experience and present my interpretation. this book, the most revealing and authentic work i've ever created, rushed out of me almost exactly as you have it. this is me. and to me, even perfection is flawed.

i've never written a book before, let alone one of poetry. rather, i like to believe i live my life in verse. i am beginning to understand my own privilege based on gender, what i look like, where i come from, socioeconomic status, and the color of my skin. what comes with this responsibility is a chance to work even harder to attempt to be a universal voice of understanding for a generation, a positive outlet for a movement, and a source of light in even the darkest of times.

all of it is you. was conceived, mapped out, and written in forty-five days. i'm not saying this for praise but rather to let you in on the process. i split the book into three sections: body, earth, universe. i wanted to start at the beginning, so i began quite literally with the origins of life, inception and birth, and through the three sections, the poems take you on a journey through human life and connection to the world around us, and finally to the universe and beyond. and strangely enough, throughout the entire writing process, i never deterred from the original order.

you will notice as you read through this book, the voice evolves. the writing of this book was a transformational journey for me, as i hope it will be for you. that's the practical magic in it. we as human beings, on this earth orb blasting through space at ridiculous speeds, are constantly trying to decipher who we are and what our voice is. i'm here to remind you, its ok, honorable even, to always, always be a work in progress. try it all, see what works, what doesn't, and know that all of it is worth celebrating because in fact, all of it is you.

i encourage you to read this book however you feel inclined. beginning to end, end to beginning, or even ask the book a question, open it to a random page and read what the book has for you. i can't promise each piece will resonate, but i can promise there is real, direct from source alchemy present on every single page. it's up to all of us, myself included, to put it to use.

before you start, a note on the cover. the six-pointed star historically carries a lot of weight. in different parts of the world, the universal shape is referred to as merkaba. *mer* meaning light, *ka* meaning spirit, and *ba* meaning body. it is known both as the chariot and the throne of god. it is believed by some to be the sacred geometry in which all life stems. for mystics around the planet, the shape has been used both for ascending and descending to dimensions other than the one we are all familiar with. for me, there's divine reason it keeps showing up in my meditations and waking life. it is the vehicle that delivers the message as far and wide as it possibly can. combined with an iteration of da vinci's *vitruvian man*, which is based on the same shape, my own natal astrology chart, our planet, the cosmos, and my left hand, hopefully there's enough power on this cover to send you everywhere.

because remember,
all of it is you
and
i love all of it,
no matter what,
all of you.

body.

sperm.

olympic medalled swimmers
fate meddling
ejaculated.
their pistol shot fired to ocean
great.
millions maybe billion
skinny dipped, iron manned
competitors, salt watered
marathoning.
seed seeding seeking
life force on nature's course.
wondering if you all play for
the same team
and the one who's strongest,
agilest butterfly stroke triumphs gold.
opportune metamorphosis.
bloom.

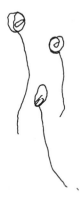

egg.

you were a good egg until you
dropped.
cycled.
fell hard for you were unused.
born eager to a flock
two million deep.
population dwindled
with each passing full moon.
alive in optimism
of meeting your landscape architect
tailed knight neoprene wet suited.
fertilized future seen.
walls porous penetrable anticipating their arrival.
all you want is to provide home.
in love. home grown.
willing to die for soul's mate.
body guards till you martyr.
created to procreate first you or the chicken.

conception.

primordial big bang.
explosion.
gospel choir worked in fireworks
fired lurks beneath your concept. ticking time
bomb counting down
till the millisecond is justified surprised.
loves landmine.
conceptualized
in mind's bodied eyes.
from where all things come, you are
my beginning.
the original expansionary idea.
infinite possibility.
finite probability.
casted offerings blasted off.

womb.

the muted tones of your room
toned beat through fluids flow.
abode.
gestated apartment
forty-week lease stated
mother grown.
positioned fetal limbs drawn in
head bows to your sacred walls.
temple zone.
i imagine you today as i go to sleep
and hear the waves moan.
always just a memory away me be phone home.

birth.

peaceful,
solitude.
calmness before the stormy mess.
souls contract. contraction.
it hurts them, it hurts them, it hurts them.
wondering if the land just split, earthquaked.
that was weird, back to sleep.
dipped contraction.
it hurts them, it hurts them, it hurts them.
and again, it stopped.
contraction.
dial eight wait nine one one.
dilate. earthquake.
light at the end of the tunnel begins to appear.
darkness obliterates.
you are the process.
head drop pop.
whose hands are those?
slip slop.
baby out peace out.
vision tunneled.
placenta plopped sacked chord cut shocked
shortcut ass smacked ok stop.
screams of joy implied babe's scared.
brand new life.
birthed.
dared.

breath.

paced changed depending on how i feel.
i need nothing more
like i need my next you.
i volunteer for you. are you voluntary?
chosen breath.
if i cognitively reminisce
time spent true
it seems but why only then?
friend cycled counted.
inhaled expansion
exhale detoxified expulsion.
building mansions in chest equipped dungeon.
how must you work when i sleep?
the diffcrence between breath and breathe.
you and me.
do i really only choose you when i remember?
only think to see you when you freeze?
like ex-lovers' hearts remorse begging please?
still so much to learn. life giving life's force.
i don't want to have to force you to keep me alive.
short of you.
i'm sorry for smoke's choke.
one day maybe one day breathe ease. deep.
so, breathe. in. out.
the reason i have to catch you
when i fall in love.

blood.

you got a bad rap.
skin wraps a gallon and a half
typed passed down and colored blue
till bled scarlet bleed.
red cells and vampire whites
suck buy and sell quality.
royal bloodlined.
hearts pumped punctual deliveries.
plasma health screen needled virus carrying tested.
donated but only by the "bested."
related by you
not always familied.
runs through veins
does not dictate crimson loyalties.
rare meats drip seas.
bloodstained splattered crime scened.
holy wine the you of christ
if i drank a case i'd be begging on my knees
please keep you clean.
spilled keep me clean.
fortunate i can wash my hands of you.
one day bloody some way maybe
the stains of their ancestors won't be permanent.

dna.

genetic coded deoxyribonucleic acid floated.
spiraled doubled helix polymer.
winding roads of maps past known.
story telling coated codes told.
you to you.
flamingo to flamingo.
toad to toad.
you make species known to the naked eye.
biological instructions function bold.
reproductions
building blocks
geometrized sacred cries.
you are what makes
lovers love
and
liars lie.

gender.

ultrasounded mars and venus.
vagina to penis.
male and female, we've seen this in you.
in between mr. to miss spectrumed.
intersexualed. chromosome mapped,
gonad internal and external.
terrestrialed extra.
bathroom segregated.
the space between the binary
socially constructed.
galaxied.
cloud pinks and blues trusted but i stand for the
rainbow in you and all its hues.
sexualed intersectional.
inclusively lived intrinsic.
what i fight for.
respect in full.
every color of you
beautiful.

name.

you are an offering to us all.
born labeled into legacy.
given mine straight off the boat.
nicolo luigi tortorella gifted you me nico for
short. niconiconico
contorted holy trinitied.
mother's maiden pesce.
italian for fish.
father's tortorella turtle dove.
hope.
genesis one-twenty-one so god created the great
creatures of the sea according to their kinds and
every winged bird in sky in their kinds
mind's eye
and god saw that it was good.
my name lands yet i come from the fishes and
the birds.
and god saw indeed that you are good.

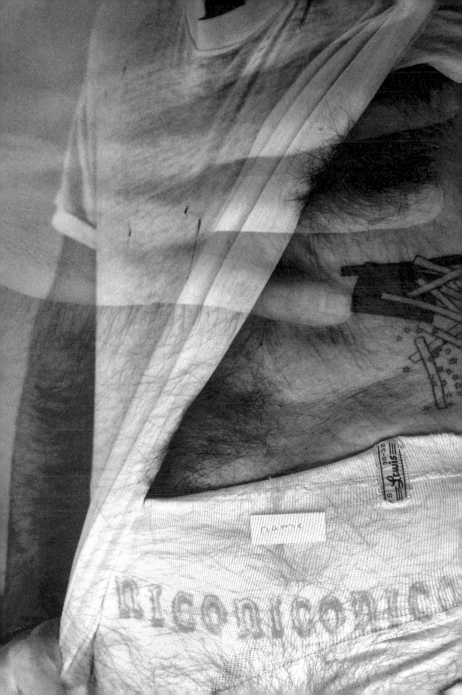

male.

physical form majoritively
masculine but not limited.
power to my femmes.
not just characteristically bold in vigor
but soft and sistered.
powered patriarchal on top
ruler measured by size and stature.
you wait for voice and balls to drop
once a boy not yet a man.
a gentleman is real man gentled.
we have to start teaching our boys to cry.
you can play ball and still weep streams.
the bully is taught broken.
i can't help but believe
there are good ones still cisgendered.
great ones role modeled. sons
and fathers brothers uncles and grands grand with
desire to protect the space of all.
a real man is a woman who wears part of himself
on the outside for the world to see.

female.

i hope the future really is you.
not soft, but softer.
alternative mainstreamed left sided divinely
feminine.
a woman is a man with whoa.
exponentially deeper internal seas.
wish i had a submarine
to explore your ocean floors.
smarter because she has to be.
pain tolerant.
bearer of all that is majestic.
edged and curved however you are,
however you want to be.
vulnerable empathy with force.
taught remorseful but she has nothing to
apologize for, she deserves the sorriest.
everything comes first from you.
every single one born from them.
by me she is love. loved. loving.
in the origin of power.
you are who i try to be,
feminist.
you
wondered woman,
wonderful you.

them.

the space between.
if man is one and woman ten
you, to me, are two through nine so. when asked
if your pronouns are
plural
maybe it's complimented.
as above, so below.
possibilities infinite.
balancing on tight ropes
trying to balance the
hes and shes or lack theres of.
if i were to say i believe we are all closer to
them, would you believe me?
you are all of it,
even if you think you're none of it.
if the immediate future is female,
the real future
i'm quartetted jazzed for
is yours.
well,
theirs.

ask for pronouns.

mother.

mommy, mother, mom.
energetically the first and last in book.
physically first and last that calls.
leos lioness
caressed cub.
first great love you taught me how greats love.
dynamic.
came from you.
stronger strength and weakened. securities and
insecurities bled. every award blessing curse
challenge in part pieced of you.
product of her but not exclusively hers.
generationally separated
ideologies.
independent normals relative.
hers traditionally formal,
well sort of.
i like to pretend i don't need you to understand
who i am, who i love
i like to pretend i have boundaries,
but build walls crumbled with mommy i love yous.
only wish is that you're always proud not of me
but of yourself and the magic that you created.
create.
this book may not be for you
but it is because of best friended you.
everything mommy
all of it is you.

father.

this may be the hardest to write,
and i know it's not your fault.
the one i stem from not always there
but i know i am offsprung
in the way my fingers flare, my
weird tongue, in the way i cross my legs.
in the depth of my love. you have one of the
greatest light gold twenty-four carat curated
loved lights but only when it's flip switched on.
stationary yet mines a vehicle that blasts off but
without yours i would have never known how to fly.
and to the one that stepped to the plate, stepped
up, mom's mary and your joseph space. my blue-
blooded king you joke but true i believe. you are
royal and i will always bend a knee and head
bow to your selfless grace.
if joseph sacrificed two doves for mary's
pregnancy, you rescued both tortorella turtle
doves. cyclical.
to every single dad in the world, you are not
always wrong. you did everything exactly the
way it was supposed to be done for all of us to
be all that we are and when the day comes
that i become one of you,
i will be made true.
tears dropping on the keyboard
as i pound keys
to hearts not yet open.

sibling.

no other loves as deeply as my brother.
same mother, same father's different ideals,
ways we play, charts planetary houses of wheels
spinning at shifted velocities.
honestly sometimes i question the capacity
at which he need, breathe, see, restrict, free.
my little brother is magic, pure unadulterated
sometimes clouded by substance and love's
abundance. speaks in waking life and dreams
in different languages.
always thinking higher, highest, wild
notions of thought, wondering "what if a dolphin
crashed into the ceiling right now?"
the boy believes, with a sparkle in his soul that
could set the world on fire if only he knew how
to strike his match. see said matchbook is wet,
been out in the rain, just waiting to dry but the
sun is out. little brother syndrome in the shadows
of my symphonies.
i the blind composer and he the one that sees.
time to let the matchbook dry and set a blaze.
my sorcerer brother,
what to do if a dolphin crashed through the
ceiling? you say a prayer, jump on her back,
matchbook in hand, ride her through the streets
lighting up every face you see.

and for the half siblings and stepbrothers,
believe parts of you mine and parts of me yours
and that's more than enough for me
to love we.

family.

tonight was thanksgiving
giving thanks at tables round.
once annually we gather chicagoed
knowed once we gathered more.
the tribe i was born some others cored.
we laughed to faces hurt
grandma swears on evil eyed and sailor swears
most.
see myself in each of you aunts and uncles older
cousins younger look to me for i don't know but
they look now not at the black sheep but at white
horse. stallioned race coursed. the one from the
other side coming home knowing not most but
some less some more.
i speak of new divinity, new york citied, new
me, polyamory, new car, new house knew not
boast.
i play cards gin rummied, taking money, raising
glasses making toasts.
block we grew up on you nurtured the boy to
man, bread to toast.
not burnt but hardened by lessoned messaged
beauties gross.
this is my home not localized
but in your eyes i know i am home in all of you.
may not all agree politically but i'm grateful for
space to be seen.
son brother nephew grandson cousin loving
blooded relative given whole. family old and new.
bloodied and chosen. all of it is you.

friend.

sometimes i wish i had more of you.
as i wander through scenes cliqued,
i wonder why aren't i cut for that life?
better one on one i suppose.
some of you outgrew.
some of you lost and found
some black and blued.
the ones i call when i don't know what.
you are counted on, secrets keeping non-
judgmental seeing all of me.
fills parts needed.
advancing, maturing.
mental capacities mattering more.
friended on media sociable
like like like like double tap swipe like.
playmated
classmated
schoolmated
workmated
soul mated
is a friend still just a friend if you've mated
conjugally?
benefited.
sex and family exclusive of you? don't think so,
you are all friends of mine
even if i don't like you
because there's still something to learn, teach
and that is to me what a friend is for.
befriended.
sport. be friend. the end.

heart.

tick tick tick tick
boom
involuntary vitality
metronomed
this achy breaky you is more than systems built
to live and built to break.
from you we feel chest
weighted chest.
tick tick beat beat
timed and rated.
from where all life is pumped
and all goes.
from where love knows love shows.
ripped mine out cold bare handed
to glow for the world needs
more light blown bypassed.
use yours to know.

by last flows beat beat flows.

liver.

you begged me to stop drowning you
so i did.
pleaded.
took a couple tries
your honor
forgive me
for years abused
filtering
devil's juice.
i loved you even
when blind to show it.
you survived fermented.
sobered three years and change
changes.
freedomed
freed of pain dumb.

you begged me to stop drowning you
so i did
and
what doesn't kill
you makes you
better
now
because of it.

brain.

winded minded.
beauty and you.
left to right draw right to write.
three pounds your mysteries greatest
for mystery created by you.
cerebrum cerebellum brainstem
all of it is, lives in, you.
where creationism and evolution met meets
knew news.
skilled motor driving force cruise controlled.
cognitive. imaginative. intuitive. emotive.
sensory sensitive. language. creative.
aggregated goods and bads.
conscious to subconscious.
memorized maybe chosen.
internal libraries entirely. physical libraries
created from you. possibilities. possibly one
hundred billion neurons one hundred trillion
connections making connections.
grecian athenaeum rows command centered
all we feel think and do.
power advanced by use. smart street to book.
knowledge actualized intellectualized. every
thought stems brain stemmed.
the difference between intelligence, intellect
and intuition is in in fact how it makes you feel.

lungs.

lying in bed with a lover
i am rocked to sleep by yours
winds sailed ships at sea.
double bubbled inflatable balloons
you mucused mucked.
two halves of heart split flipped housing airs
out
in.
bronchial trees bloomed upside down
to lobes superior and inferior.
tombed.
where oxygen goes to die carbon dioxide out
zooms. respiratory gas exchanged storied over
and over the years i've blackened you, blew
smoked from cigarettes camel blue to organic
hand rolled american spirited mapacho.
the left you may be smaller than the right you
making space for hearts but i love you both the
same. flawed love but true. hurt you with fags
fogs smogged exhaust polluted campy fire but
when i quit smoking you'll have time to heal and
in healing you'll know what feeling better feels
like.
never again like new but healing.
you rise and fall
just like the rest of them.
it is when you stop all together
then all else fails.

stomach.

relationship toxic
with appearance external.
hair like paternal.
why it is i feed off skin tight slick to muscle
bone seen packed eight never maybe five and a
half though photoshopped better.
dysmorphic though at least i know it.
trying to love you all ways better
even if i can't
find ways to show it.
however
internally
the difference between sick
and housing butterfly's monarchs is lined fine.
sick to my stomach from the butter fights
fly butterflights
where caterpillars grew cocooned.
are you hungry
loud
or just craving attention?
are you the real route to man's heart and
woman's too? i always like you better empty
anyway. more room for the social butterflies to
take wing.

skin.

cut and sew yourself
back together you are magic.
however, toned problematic.
comfortable
in my own you privileged
yet uncomfortable with it.
if beauty is only you deep
i'm not interested.
i want what you house.
no one ever should really care
about its shutters.
you're cute and all
glowing tissue
layers epidermis dermis.
thick
you firmed this issue.
but if thick skin makes
tougher tough
i don't want it.
i wish you were transparent
we could see beauty real
rather than predetermined
by history's shortcomings.
hold on the sun is coming.
let me cover before you burn
more than you already have
holes in history.

bones.

enablers.
over two hundred and seventy
pushing us
mobile
cells red white produced.
i've got a you to pick with you.
why are you the only thing that stays alive
when we die?
our dirt is made of your macabre.
wonders who decided our skulls would be
symbols of mortality. in reality
to be or not to be
is not the question but the backbone.
can we be and not be at the same time?
that is the answer.
choking on wishbones making wishes
a wish is reality seen
glistening in a future
actualized
no need to break you in half
to decide.
it's funny though the funny bone.
who came up with you?
bone backbone back to bone.
wait,
who decided to make love was to bone?
good luck out there.
break a leg.

face.

you are either a great liar
or the worst in the world.
honest there is no in-between where secrets kept
freed.
where you become you.
where me is me.
recognized.
alterable
but your kids will always be born
with your old nose.
wrinkles scars battles laugh attacks. memorized
but sometimes needle filled with new memories.
with country and city miles per gallon relative.
beauty apparently mathematically proportionate
but i want to know how your expression lights.

life is always better face to face. you to you.
seen.

eyes.

open up.
mines vision of the world
not better
but different.
seen unique sheens.
one eye to the sky
one to the ground,
tarot magician.
physically i see you
in the mirror reflected.
vision paired
less than twenty twenty
lazy eyed tear duct blocked
vision impaired.
seen through collectors of lightness. optimum
optical looks past what you see.
seeing is believing in believing
and a you for a you make you blind.
what color are you really if no two the same
fingerprinted?
i can see the universe in you through you.
blasted images relative to how they
affect brain's function.
what you see is not all you get.
do you remember what color mine are or
were you not paying attention? head cock slow
blink. tears drop. eye contact i connect.
if i the apple in yours
i want your entire garden in mine.
closed. sleep. dream.
open up.

nose.

knows you as nose.
mine tip heart shaped dipped proportioned.
center staged faced care bared. cockeyed.
pick you for breathing
smelling clearly unobstructed.
trim your hairs as scaped.
perplexed by your smell
if you're for smelling do you have one too?
scents of direction.
keep yours in my business,
as mines shared.
geographically scouted by shapes snouted.
if you're too high
i can't see where i'm going.
nasal pitched
fumes to cavities
deep. sinus
disadvantaged clogged minus
knowing which perfumes in rooms
smell familiar.
blow you clear,
sometimes all we need in life
is a good blow.

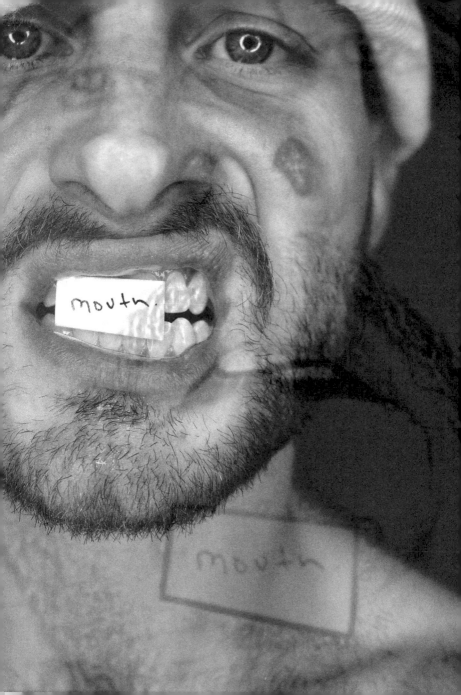

mouth.

the lips the teeth the tongue
the tip of the iceberg.
the first based opening.
the kiss.
frenched sensual.
the bite chewed lick the honey from my
chapsticked.
gums salivate masticated big chews gum.
nobody should really put their money where you
are unless its gold. unsanitary exchange makes
you stronger. vaccinate.
moods smiles mile long to
bumper lip frown.
tongues sprung gloried for more of the spit of
the gods.
feast upon my whole face holies hole.
feed on bee's knees suckle marrow sucked.
mom stuck thermometer to check dragon's fire
breathed.
eat meat and slurp orchids juice flowered.
molars canine's incisors.
drool for the sweet fool
but swallow the sage.
run off big you.
i'll always keep watching and washing.
don't you dare shut up
unless
you need more time to think.

ears.

listen hear bucko.
(drumroll please)
you decide
deduced what is music to you
and what is simply noise.
noise black
and white noise
misconstrued.
symphonic to token spoken hooked on phonics.
if foreign language just goes in one of you and
out the other why can i still feel it?
you keepers of balance.
to be honest you pair are the weirdest
looking things we got
shaped swirly twirled parts out.
channeling channels to dome too loud drums
blown. loud noises loud noises shock. whispers
kiss her sweet nothings. the sound of a mother's
voice lovers noise. listen to me even if you
don't like what i'm saying.
there's a message in it.
the voice inside your head is always the loudest.
listen to them. the voice
inside your head is always the loudest.
the reason why listen and silent have the same
letters contained rearranged.

hands.

to touch is to feel
and i love feelings.
dominant dexterous right-handed demands, and
takes while
left forgives for giving.
one for myself and one for others.
you give yours to theirs,
holding tight.
electric explosions.
some say our entire machine pointed in points
pressure pressed ology reflexed.
paired sets of five.
two thumbs up opposable.
index scanners.
middle fingers raised in protest.
rings for wed.
pinky's not always pink toned flesh. nailed.
caliced worn.
palms get sweaty clammed but if i love them i'd
still hold theirs.
mystics palms read lifelined.
prints of fingers exclusive.
high fived prayer
higher ten in god's eyes. tactile.
come together in celebration, victory.
using you to create handmade.
lust over wrinkles and veins.
you hold the power to destroy manipulate or give
love thanks.
the choice is in yours
the beholder.

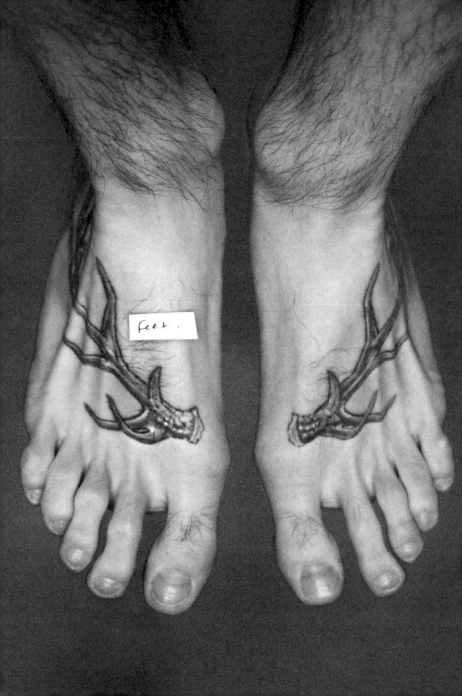

feet.

i may
walk all over you
but
i swear
you're the only ones
that keep me
standing.

navel.

i have one spot on my body
that is always off limits
belly buttoned not for pressing.
i'm sure there's a deeper energy
at work
to learn
but for now,
you'll keep collecting lint
and i'll
do my best to keep you safe
you sensitive
loner you.

penis.

cauterized at birth
circumcised,
an ancient covenant fulfilled
but still, i wish
you were uncut, natural, organic, hooded
protected.
they say orgasms would be better.
more like hers blows bright, redder.
organ veined, hung low
unless you're cold

a well-versed verse cavern traveler,
mines average, ridden and rode,
the only skin that's rubbed more than hands.
grower, grow for show.
pistol whips you sure have reputations
sized and timed.
of your own mind.
nonjudgmental unless more drunk or powdered
snort drugged.
mine beauty marked and
if birthmarks are god's touch then i'm fully
touched blessed be thy holy touch.

weapon and medicine.
not a man for you, but more of a man because
of the relationship, relationships
complexed by you,
with you.

testicles.

a man
is not
defined by you.
but if you
the most sensitive two
i have,
i guess it may
just take the thought
of you
to be
a real man.

ovaries.

they say
it takes balls
nope
it takes you.

vagina.

bow down to the one with crown.
that crowns extraordinary.
not just for birthing.
pussy powered conjured country.
grounding.
right. deserving rights
earthing.
searching for discoveries
unearthing truth.
pissed
sacred lips.
clitoris.
kiss consensual.
floral.
the holy ghost orchid.
get lost and found in your raw chocolate cosmos.
parrot's beak speaking truths.
champion's campion.
yellow and purple
lady slippers
to keep warm.

swallow me whole
and
take me to your leader.

menstruation.

cycle mimicking lunars
merry go rounds earth phase.
hormones wax and wane.
uterine lines thicken with drop of egg.
if said roe missed encounters with soul's mate,
you show up to sage clear space.
blood outflows.
tampons and pads and cups in size grow.
life's cycle begins again.

bleed ten to eight milliliters a week.
every month.
ages span varied.
getting heavier in the developed world
everything else alike.
the pill can regulate.
four hundred and fifty cycles in a lifetime.
average rate.

that's roughly eleven thousand pads sanitary for
your all one's born days.
close to seventy thousand dollars paid.
i can still wipe my ass for free publically.
tampons and pads should be chargeless.
comped.
our eggs should have more equity than our
shit.

you are even more beautiful when you bleed
complimentary.

nipple.

only his are freed.
the fight for equal nudity.
hers may one day children feed
so, giving life is more controversial?
politicized, sexualized, demonized,
censured, censored on social media feeds.
social rules piercing cold
make it harder to touch.
men sexualize everything free
desexualize the female version
women won't be constantly objectified.
none of you are free
until
all of you are free.

breast.

curving bosom,
utterly beautiful
i could
run up and down your hills
until breathless
big and small though prefer you smaller
natural to augmented.
alphabetized sized.
some caught
busted staring
boobs.
proof focusing
on more than one thing
at a time is possible.
bra,
bro,
just a tad higher
you'll be better off locking eyes.

ass.

i can kiss you and make things
better.
i can kick you and make things
better still.
i can be a bad you and look cooler.
i can even eat you whole,
honey baked
without shame.

but if i'm hard or smart,
i'm an asshole
screw you.

the difference between an ass and a stallion is
only in the way you hold yourself.

armpit.

i've always loved
lover's smells.
pheromones
scented signals
attracted.

diving head first
to the pits of them
arms if it meant
i could swim
that much deeper
to grottos of them
souls.

i'll fly forward
one-and-a-half
somersaults, pike
however which way.
hairy shaved
sprayed odored.

just promise
i'll always have the nook
below shoulder.
to snuggle

muscles.

grow when
ripped and torn apart,
bigger from the strain,
stronger from adversity.
focused on.
armstrong stretched to limits
pushed, burnt.
better for it.

six hundred and forty
actively built and toned,
mightier strength.

if left alone you weaken, atrophied
non trophied.
don't ever neglect the ones
you love even the ones disagreed.

maybe sore today but
tomorrow is always new.
moneyed meats water and honey
feed.

your ability to heal depends on how well we take
care.

nerve.

it takes you to be bolded.
system mapped, fibers bodily webbed.
brain and spinal cord central databased.
peripherally axoned
you shoot to every single part
of the body.
sans you, every macro system to micro cellular
workings immobile.
the remote controller to my television
sending signals
to change the picture.

if you do it all
why is being nervous
considered a flaw?
i work better under viscerally responsive
responsibility.
the split between nerve and nervous
is in the choice of the shell.
the line between nervous and awakened is fine
and fragile.

when nervous it means the time for
enlightenment is near. awake.
use nerve and embrace.

at the end of the day i'd rather feel everything
than nothing at all and that's on you.

endocrine.

system's secret hormones, secreted by glands
planned function may just hold the direct
connection to source.
the contracted compass of contact
between body mind and spirit.
to bring us closer to god.
fact gland pineal is your
original state of construction.
from where all embryos begin
and all go to sleep.
hypothalamus in charge.
life's proprietary pituitary.
salivary salivates.
prostate orgasmed sends sea men's on voyage.
mammary for milk and honey.
thyroid void of action unless action is taken.
thymus heart centered open.
according to plato soul's home.
pancreas insulates blood's insulin.
adrenals adrenaline centered
emotional life pumped.
testes and ovaries motored energy.

you are affected by how we feel, all of you.
aggression delivers health's regression. positive
thought learned and taught heals positively.
manifest flight.
the butterfly effect is real.

hair.

the way you lay on my chest worthy swoon.
on top of my head your greatest city.
population: one hundred thousand, give or take
dependent on color.
blondes have the most to have more fun.
as puberty goes hair grows in spots known.
binary split with loads of exceptions considering
where dna stemmed.
geographically specific however as cultures
blend so do trends deemed appropriate.
racially defined.
religiously inclined.
bought and sold like gold.
styled bold. bush is beautiful.
cut colored curled limped primped beards oil
smeared crimped wigged rigged ironed flat
straight shaved barbers blades dreads heads beds
bald pompadoured tall.
sprouts in ears nose protect dust blown.
never look past a good lash or brow.

from samson to becky
and every strand in between.
i love the way you continue to grow
even though i keep cutting you with blades.
just don't ever ask to touch anyone's.

sweat.

drip drip drop.
gather in puddles but i won't drown
rather i can breather deeper under your streams.
beads that melt when worn hard and glisten hot.
emotionally reactive.
fear not.
wealthy himilayan salted waterfalls evaporate to
thermoregulatory expectation.
that cool cooling bodies cooler.
wetting sweating skins lubed pops from
cleansing innards that showers can't wash.
when i was drunk
you used to show up in my sleep.
the sixth lake great.
as a nightmare or dream i can't quite see
but i know
the only monster loch ness in your seas was me
and if it weren't for you keeping me afloat
in hope
i'd already be belly up or
six feet deep

piss.

the way
you flow
hued canary.
coloring is
hydrates gauge,
tickled tinkled
when my grandma laughs.
whizzed from tunnels
spiraled metabolic
liquid tonic.
first to wake up
good mornings
final resting room
before
times night.

pained fight
in my bladder
the worst
though
always looking for
a toilet
tree
or
street without police
(that ticket's expensive),

and i love when it's cold outside.
i can see your heat
as i sign my name
in the white snowed sleet.

shit.

everyone
is
full of you.
grace
is in
how well
you
move true.

orgasm.

are you the end result or just the beginning?

my body longs for you.
hardened shaft longer than rested,
although i've been known to find you softed.
meditative swelling. processed.
cosmic muscles spasm rushed oxytocin prolactin
endorphins.

it's true it takes two to tango
but only one to break dance
and my worm whistles more like dolphin.
not quite sure if you are solely mine or the
precursor for new soul's flight.
whether you the cause for more ecstasy or
headaches.
everyone is different.
phallic wick quicker runs out delicious.
if i could run a mile
in clitoris currents charged,
would i fabricate crossing the finish line?
would the victory dance last longer stronger?
for now i'm more than happy aiding watching
and waiting till rosebuds ignite.
you are the end of passion's ascension,
just as you are the beginning
as i still have to climb back down
from your peak.

chakras.

the real seven wonders of my world.
spinning me right and left round baby wheeled
right round. rainbowed flowed.
rooted in red.
sacral sacreds orange.
flex this solar plexus mellow yellow.
hearted clean greens.
throat to speak blue royally.
third eye glows indigo.
golden crown violet gemmed.

energetically centered.
vibrational frequencies communicate.
centered spine base to brain to flight.

your doorways swing both ways as do i.
mandalas petals blossom all ways.
balancing always.
first foot in then all the way.

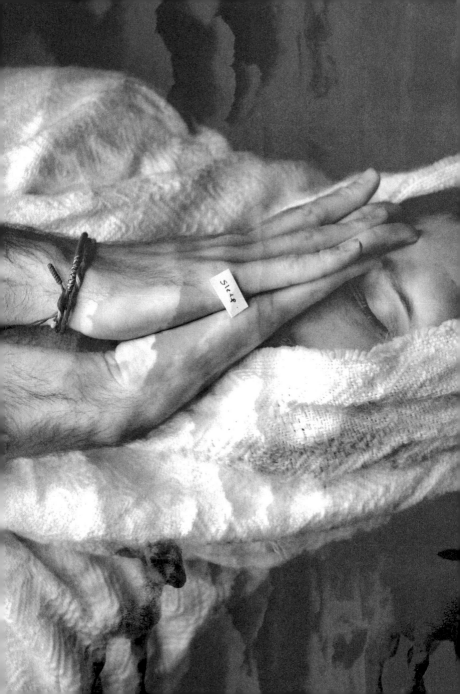

sleep.

every night i fall for you, to you.
shutting eyes, opening mouth
rolling down the meadowed slopes of linen sheets,
counting their sheep
into your waiting embrace.

every piece of you.
eyes heavy bagged up belonging cognizant.
beginning stages set for night ahead,
pillow under head and one between my legs.
deepest mariana trench wave
sweet dreams.
corneal movement eyes rapid in those moments
brain function improving.
cells repairing,
mind filing and storing all day.

if life falls apart when we wake,
you graciously give time to put the pieces back.
recharge while my phone is recharging.

dream.

sometimes i pass out wide awake just to see you.
illuminating either vigilant or asleep
a truth found.
pure creativity in imagination.
endless possibilities.

people speak of lucid dreams
when actually we are always lucid,
whether or not our eyes are open.
being awake is lucid dream with consequence.

but you are freedom.
nothing is real.
nothing is realer.

imagine if we could film you while you sleep.
record you in some way.
rewatchable.
wait.
maybe it's already happening.

what if reality is just everyone's dreams being
replayed. and the only real nightmares are the
ones we ourselves create.

ego.

i love you
even though everyone thinks you're a dick.
you are all of it
build me up from the e go.
where it begins.

the secret is figuring out where to keep you when
the soul in steps.

never killed,
but checked.

identity.

lover, friend, boyfriend, future husband, seeker,
student, artist, singer, dancer, poet, producer,
foodie, honey loving, son, brother, grandson,
cousin, nephew, dog daddy, collector best friend,
muse and inspiration.
what defines me?
the me, programmed construct.
the personality and energy behind it.
29 years young,
on my 30th rotation around the sun.
the not so fully realized
privileged, white, italian american.
cisgender, queer, bisexual
mathematically proportioned human being.
most of the time.
my masculinity is fragile. my feminine freeing.
the recovering alcoholic who still smokes
organic tobacco. occasional psychoactive
dabbler. the diving deep into mysticism and
meditation learning what it means to be healer.
the actor, first great love.
the activist, next great love.
the actorvist, the player of words.
the frolicker. the voice on the podcast.
the celebrity.
the not this not that beyond definition.
the work in progress.
my you is me.
i am me. the i. fluidly.

expression.

ability to play.
if identity is canvas, you
the paint,
how what is inside manifests
outward.

from facial to gender to artistic to self,
creative artistry.

your own you.
the only one that knows how.
do it for yourself first
always.

tears.

you build and fall
from love and pain.
cascades down facial river beds
till you hit my lips.
i love the way you taste.
an overzealous appetite for heavy weighted
alkaline drops.

cries silent you for joys blessings.
hyperventilates for
cursed thoughts.
weeps even in deep sleeps.

manifested emotion in physical form.
always, all ways cleansing.

i may rather cry than orgasm.

occasionally
when the two
contemporaneously combust,
out of love,
in that very moment
a star illumes
and shoots through
night skies.

laughter.

the guttural response
shoulder shaking
short of breath
face stretched
every line across mine chiseled
like lovers carve names in trees
memories journaled

make it a mission to
not get out of bed
till i've heard you scream
rolling in the aisles of
white linen sheets
tumbling to floors
just you and me

you are the cure
and silly
i hope to die laughing too

no joke

higher self.

purest form,
void of fear and discretion.
the inner voice that makes all better.
the real hero super superb.

the purest bright form of light.
the captain of the ship.
intuitive. synchronistic.

once we realize abilities move past the physical
plane, we have the capacity to step into you.
now,
new skin.

never alone however lonely
at times.
the greatest present is your presence. the direct
connection to source.
the source of all that is good.

i chose you because you allow me the best
version of myself.

holy grail.

one of the greatest mysteries of human existence.
you perhaps the holiest of holy.
quested infamous.
legend has it the last supper drank from you by
jesus before judas slain.
but what if i proclaimed
there never was a holy cup
at least not the arked grail we thought saved.
but instead it may be inside our skulls
planted below brains.
bone sella turcica is said to be the seat of the
saddle housing gland pituitary.
fluids drip from pineal, a chalice holding the
fountain of youth springs sprung.

dimethyltryptamine released high dosed
when you're born, when you die,
low dosed when you sleep to dream.
the oil that runs the vehicle for multi-
dimensional travel.

what if everything we've been taught has been to
keep us dormant? shackled.

and the real you has been inside each and every
one of us all along.

sacred wine waiting to be savored to properly
blast off.

sex.

when two become one.
but if i'm already more than,
how many would you like to become?
course in her and his and their course study.
mate's coitus copulates.
come.
always come second. proper etiquette.
even though i show up for the writer first.
always.
engage with myself making holes from hands.
engage with others,
digging for gold in holes, in lands
but not on whim.
not to knock modern day swipe and swings,
but i need investment emotional pre cosmic stroll
or else my spacecraft apollo won't have the gas
to blast it.
you however are not just acts cast.
sometimes your nouns gender.
whatever.
verbs determinate.
the you with a y is sexy even phonetically.
and sometimes you mean 6 and to be honest
that's just too many to wrap my head around.
always practice safe.
not always latex cased, but a vulnerable
exchange keeping the ones you love protected.
it's hard. right now.

nico tortorella

sexuality.

the spectrum so wildly vast
there is in no way you always walk a distinctly
straight line.
at one point, we even thought earth was flat.
indeed, is round.
you are galaxies infinite,
gravitationally pulled.
and i believe in every one
of your planetary iterations
heteros is greek for different?
sexuality assigned only by the human,
we are born to appreciate differently,
a spectrum of life
homo sapiens, wiser men than to continue to
break it down and label it
if sex is what we do, and you what we are,
choose to not define myself by acts loved crude.
choose to be defined by how i love myself first,
then my ability to love all.
sexuality without sex rather love
is the duality perfectly balanced.
masculine and feminine.
the tree of life.
nonjudgmental. freedom.

health.

when i carry you, i have everything
and barely pay attention.
take your wealth for granted.
expect you.
wish i didn't.

you are not only
what i eat.
you are what i believe.
and i believe in you.

if i lose you
i lose everything

illness.

broken down, unable.
battling bacteria and tackling everyday criteria.
sick. but somehow, every time i pull through and
wonder the purpose lessoned.
to breath and stop and pray,
to light the candle from one end only.

fighting. fought hard to get here
harder to stay alive,
when the time is right all things must die.
is that you that finally wins?
you the low energy piece of
trying to distract me from living
full potential at hand.
and if on the other end come out,
wear scars as armor bullet proofed as pride is
proof we're still alive.
no matter what illness physical or mental,
refuse defeat

emotion.

stemming from memories deep rooted
you stirred up viscerally remind me of something
that happened in passing's past, which leads to
the now response. body, conscious responsive,
energetically sensory active in motion from
subconscious gas.

the fifth state that starts with i. instinct.

i wear you on my sleeve in not so muted tones
mooded circumstantial.
occasionally without reason.
not so uncontrollable but i prefer your course
run through completion.

i feel you in everything
but choose which to focus.
cyclical in nature.
feeling one extreme
for the lesson in its adversary.
somber taught bliss, chaos directs peace.
accordingly, paradoxical.
all equally important as one does not exist
without its counterpart.

you remind me to truly live, thrive, in the
moment however painful or pleasant emotive
trust over logics must.

question.

mark my words.
to seek
is to see.
k?

truth.

you are subjective to perspective.
"your honor, objection."
yells the man of god.

dimensional dependent.

nonfiction's afflictions stranger than the
alternative's infliction.
moral fidelity.
i demand you.

if you can really set us free,

god we need you. now.

lie.

apparently in today's world you can
flaming hot cheeto spit fire from tongues like
devils drooling on truths.
he should be hung. the devil that is.

realities alternate.
for you have the power to skew. fabricate your
own fake news.

i fear not the disease of your seeds however
worse than plagues. for as you continue to
sprout, so do we.

engaged in rage.

make america true again.

love.

the verb, the noun, the adjective.
you are the practice
as much the game.
as passive as you are active.
healing as you are explosive.
habitual as revolutionary.
unknown as all knowing.
conditional as unconditional.
rejecting as accepting.

the fabric of life,
even though i prefer to be naked,
you the complex damask weave
that i blanket tightly around bare shoulders.

projected abilities only as loud and wide as you
scream for yourself.
ears to hear, eyes can see.
you are the mirror mirror and i the hearted ace
king joker and queen.

if i loved you once, i love you forever
even if it breaks.
if our love's scorn torn apart that does not
definitively implicate failure.
story booked it wasn't you, it's me.
i needed more time to love myself.
falling to get back up.

hate.

hate you.
mean it.
literally.

good.

all that is you in the world is invariably right.
better than acceptable. exceptional.
the proudness in morality.
the fist in the air to fight for this
righteousness,
rights for this, for justice, for peace.
the striving, imagination to seek,
hug a friend in need or even spontaneously.
the you egg hatches vibrating bright white light
at highest frequencies
neat light on all around to bask superbly
satisfactory, sterling quality tip tops the top
of the tips top of the morning to day you night.
you the job and the measure.
as you as it gets as you as new

you are worth it
of it first rate
you are worthy.

evil.

lowest of energy takes the most to spew.
villainous.
terrified of light's exposure.
beastly poison corrupts for the sake of power
you eyed uglied.
maleficent malevolent malicious repugnant
monstrosities.
mug the twin to strip bare the wicked atrocities
and still underneath masked goblins pure
innocence beautiful i'm sure.

money is not the root of all you, rather how
earnt to spent.

i'm convinced there is more good
than you in the world and we accept
the divine responsibility cast upon
the best to take you out.

fantasy.

you are not reality's escape method
rather the only sure way to capture it
as to flavored savor this captivity.

happiness.

not needing you, not expecting you
is the only way to find you truly.
it's not about asking, buying, taking, trying
but the journey trek oregon trailed taken to get
there was the happy one, where it comes from.
not needing anything at all is when i am truly
happiest.

pain.

a warning,
danger messaged.
the indication a lesson
it should be better, you are.

forgiveness.

forgive yourself
for everything that is.
for giving
amnesty as
you are more than worth it.

doesn't need to apologize
for me to see
that
he is sorry.

glad i the power
to have forgiven
his error
mortal
as i'm more
easily intrigued
in
being
celestial.

victory.

to win is to lose a piece of myself that was no
longer serving.
whether it be catastrophically pyrrhic or
landslide flawless.

goals lead to you.
and you
my friend
are goals.

loss.

at a you for words
to know
the strength
in realizing
once gone
how much it was worth.

cut your yous
sever
to play
to gain
again.

purpose.

stumbled accidentally on you and delivered me
reason for all existence.

the world needs more
the trick is living with you
and never having
to worry about
money.

desire.

i
want all of you
earthly
otherworldly

i'm starving

yearning for
your
beating hearts
consumption

always i lick
the plate clean.

addiction.

barely woke in mornings
bed wet
from
nights binged
the pain still
lingering

stumbled to freezer
iced wet vodka bottle glass
swigged down like
fast water
stomach burns like warm hugs
from the inside
by beast himself

doubled suckered
as punch drunk love
shot to face

three years ago divorced,
however, that love
never fades
and familiar hearts
still break
for you cause
the ache.

i used to numb the pain
before i knew
to heal

drink.

i drink to make myself more interesting.

vegetable and fruit
juice cold pressed
vitamixed
nuts milk
milked coconuts
kombucha ferments
apple cider vinegar
turmeric and ginger
grasses wheat
coffee organic tea
cacao hot and cold
chaga lion's mane mushroom reishi
tocotrienols
mayan maca
pollen from bees
collagen infused
superfood elixirs
soy interesting
except not soy, it's 2018

i love you
responsibly

drug.

warning. this one may get you going.
quick shots montaged.
gateway mirrors railed lines snort cocaine puffed
toked ounce ice in bong pipes sativa indaca
medicinal weed and needles shoot belts tied dead
head dead eyed street corner scoring dope from
the dope man white and black tar heroin blue
meth cooked by high school profess my love for
molly has anyone seen my girlfriend molly booty
bumped comedown serotonin dumped acid tabs
popped like socks on feet time warps floor salvia
wars tile mile ketamine k special k cereal killer
milk the tree frog kambo long while i chew
fungus psilocybin sunflower gluten free
sandwiches chocolate mushroom fantasies cactus
flower potted peyote eggs cracked in pan this
your brain on drugs dead pan scrambled thoughts
out of hand oxy xan fentanyl epidemic addict
quaalude prelude rehabilitated narcotics
anonyms expansion shamanic immersion
ayahuasca ceremonies grandmother all seeing
legal high or illegally crimed
abuse you chemically to deplete
use you organically to expand
you can make or break the man
be careful with you as i'm only trying to better
understand why i'm here and why you are too

smoke.

fireborn
year of dragon
scaled fire bird
inferno flown heated

i'm a blazing

signed fire signed sealed delivered
king of the jungle
mapacho sacred tobacco
protected, in yours

your familiarity palpable
reminders signaled
from where i've spawned
heat mustered
must live on

evidently, you're not the best for me
my dear
after all fire all fire smokes
consequently
you're the closest i get to breathing flame

for now.

food.

fuel
petrol graded
dependent on
body types
desired
and model minds
as food, truly is, for thought

masticate
to taste
i crave all texture

caloric energy
enough power to destroy
from the inside out
engines internally combust

powered to heal
organically
electric cell charged

just don't piss in the tank

water.

convoy conductor
round and round it goes
gulped to flush to flush
filtered as necessary
this day and age

when it all boils down
i wish we knew to savor was to swallow
appreciatively
before we were
desperate

i love you when you sparkle for me baby
but don't be thirsty

medicine.

if laughter really is
the best you,
western doctors
and the
pharmaceutical companies
that pay them to get paid
must live forever.
laughing all the way,
back and forth,
to bank.

fitness.

billboards added to mandatorily fit this
prescribed manufactured idea of beautiful.
eat this train this diet try this quit this
to fit this suit or dress.

is the fittest the sumo biggest the flipping
gymnast the quickest mile minutes the muscled
arnold thickness the modeled railway thinness
the richness or sickness?

nutrition proper
actively prosperous
efficiently rest

you are not defined by weight carried or lifted
dropped swiftly but by carrying oneself to better
care for oneself.

sport.

life is not raced against each other
per contra, raced against time
a good you can accept the loss head high

except in the colosseum
as the loser commonly died
head spiked
blown the competition away
striker

time out

i suppose that's why
in this stage of the game
we call the defeated yet
still alive
good sports

pointed

so, give it your best shot kid
just don't go overboard

thanks, coach
how much time is left on the clock?

clothing.

i may wear you out
performative in nature
urban jungled
dressed to live
eclectic

vintage spirit spirits relived
with tricks seemingly sleeved
hard-on for the hearts on
victorian hand sewn
forever flown
by pants seats
down buckled
i swear

when hats drop
(i have thousands)

if i could
imagine the crusade
of every galosh
pilgrimaged
boots
ever worn
put myself in shoes
miles and miles trekked known
without exception

only then
only then
will i keep my shirt on

communication.

read between the lines

---

the art of you is key

---

express oneself
unlock the doors
contact
connection
intercourse

let it out
because if you don't,
it shits inside.

activism.

don't have to
see something
to say something
to do something.

your voice matters,
while
your actions effect,
abled glass shatter.

language.

six thousand nine hundred and nine
of you,
and only one universally that matters:
love.

relationship.

cosmic law
ruled platinum
they will treat others
the exact way
they trick and treat themselves

fall in love with yourself to fall in love with
them.

or at least
to know
if they're worth it.

marriage.

i have issue with you
inequality speaking
the piece of paper
benefits reaped decidedly
archaic laws set by church
still directly connected to states
not just nationally
and why does sickness come before health
vowed?
and why are we talking about death at a time like
this?
symbolic exchange
a ring energetically protecting the one finger
veined directly to heart
i've spent the last eleven years
in one way or another
with my best friend
and plan to spend the next
hundred lifetimes with them, so
bethany christene meyers
all of it is, has always been, always will be, you.
i love you.
as i get down on one knee as to bow in your
presence.

will you marry me?

except i have issue with even that tradition. so,
we had a conversation and mutually agreed the
time is now to tie the knot, as that's how it
should be. bye patriarchy.

children.

i have dreamt of you. already held you in arms
and wept. woke in mornings more whole except
without you to physically hold. i hold your soul
in mine known you are already super starred
special molded from wellspring holy and
although you may hear things about mom and
dad i need you to know there has never been a
love more expansive than the one we have. till
now. you are the physical manifestation of our
explosive energy, see you hold us both entirely
forever and ever as we hold you. babies, we love
you. more than you will ever know and although
we won't be perfect and neither will you we
prefer it that way. as much as we're trying to
make this world a safer place it is still wildly
flawed so that just means there's more to play
more to work hard more to create. you my dears
are defined freedom. as lucky as we are to have
you, you are to have us wild us. unconditionally
without exceptions we accept you and the only
piece we ask in return is simple. you have been
created out of pure cosmic love, so whenever
things get tough as human beings they must
return to us exampled that love always wins no
matter what. and don't take any of it too
seriously. babies, have fun. i love you, still
dreaming of you, for you, forever with tears.
—dad

prayer.

gratitude must always come first.
grateful for the space to call on you.
beholden to the capacity at which to ask.
thankful for gratitude itself.

all that i come from, everything that we are,
everywhere that we are going.

thank you.

then ask.

speaking to him is the equivalent of speaking to
her which invariably means you're speaking to
them and if all of it is you, well, you get where
i'm going.

when you go up
blessings come down.

calling on anyone for anything is calling on
yourself to show up for the request.
the first step.

blessings in blessings in blessings
all around us.
rub my hands together, wish, rub, blow.

and thank you again
i love you amen

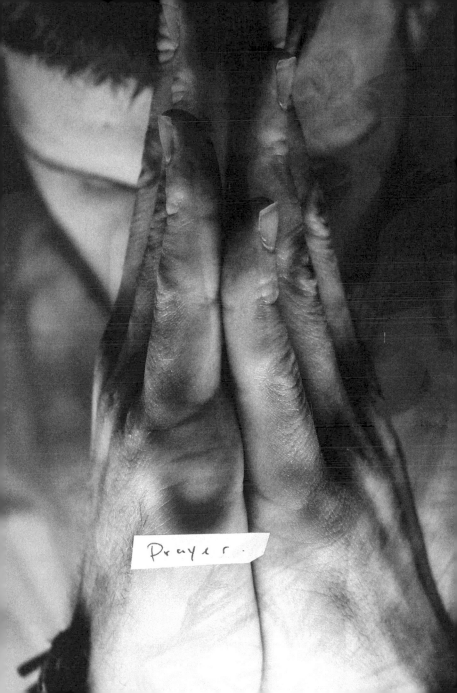

meditation.

if prayer is the chance to give thanks and ask.
you are the opportunity for them to thank us, ask
more, speak back.

guided only by your own imagination to expand
there is no right way. a deep breath collected
thoughts intentions set in and out airways.
possibilities endless. connect to spirit guides
through blasted open wide third eyes.
transformational. transcendental. travel astral.
heart beated rhythmic, visuals used to visualize
it kundalini awakens it zenned out zazen in it qi
gong mindfulness. quiet this or turn the volume
all the way up and rock in bliss.

practice it as it not to be the best version as
that implies an end result. practice to better. no
matter who you are or where you come from you
can close your eyes and take deep breaths.

in with love, out with love.
spell it. dance in it.
imagine it. ask for it. believe in it.
feel it to
see it to be it.
now for real close your eyes, ten deep breaths,
start practicing, the answers have always been
deep inside you.
up to us to close our eyes and look.

heal.

to heal, to be healed, to healer
to you, to be you, to be you-er

all are broken someway
that in essence is our universal pureness.
broken yet pure.

the art of life is in the ability to put the
pieces back together.

bodies made for you of you
machined by alleviation
reprogramming constantly
physical wounds miraculously repair
minds rewind lessoned to move forward
souls wander and perish to be reborn
heartbreak however drowned
always swims up for air
baptized in time and process

take a step back
in awe of what mosaic
you've created

all great art is troubled,
you are masterpiece

master
the
pieces.

death.

the one sure fired promise
of all that bares life,
the terribly predictable
unpredictable

i hate to see people slowly dying
killing each other
taking their own lives
simply surviving

i'm afraid of that
but i am not afraid of you.

why waste sacred life simply surviving?
make something of it

i know
all things must end,
as there would be no beginning
no middle no climax no best part no hero no love
interests no resolution no review no story no
writings on the wall no nothing
not even the end without you.
all of it leads to you
up to us to make it worthwhile

and who knows
maybe you are just the beginning in disguise.
light at the end of the tunnel is just a new—

god.

all of it
within me
is you.

earth.

land.

grass and dirt fed trees to flower bedded moss to
get lost and found
sanded graveled sediment sentiment
to fall to knees and kiss you. grounded.
i land on you
land for your catch to trusts fall
crawl and walk and run for you bounce
ascension from your power washed floors
all structure ascends from your grounds and built
of you, from your launch pad
white marble brushed enough to see
my reflection diamond invented
fermented cement cracked and if those could talk
i would listen to talk back
habitable to protected decided by men
taken advantage of
ripped and stripped of resource natural
however
you are still my favorite, every color
your beauty infinite
fully inclusive

in awe of your shapes mathematically perfectly
proportioned

i will always choose to land on you, as you will
forever catch my fall no matter how hard even
buried 6 feet ground under, even dead, blossoms
bloom, and we continue to grow for you

waters.

there has never been any more of you
than what began,
no new you.
you make up the same percentage of the planet
as you do my body,
the relationship is symbiotically intrinsic.

the great conducted current that connects us all
and sends messages cryptic
shipped round and round.

they say you are where it all began
but we know so little of your deepest intent.
freshwater we bought her bottled and pump
through systems public worked sanitary and yet
millions still don't have you clean.
basic needs.
not so sanitary
you used to run through canal streets streamed
and it all leads back to sea salted.
float on your surface when my breath is full,
sink when i'm empty.
skate on your dreams when iced hard.
inhaled steam deep.
multi formed organic

and baby when the sky opens for your rain, strip
me down, grab my hand, and run not for cover as
i'd rather be covered in you.

air.

creative flow to still.
even still you're active
swishing through time and space.
intangible but holy am i able to feel you. to
breathe you is to be alive. gasp.
run with your winds. not against it.
flags flip flap swing patriot
back stroke in your humid tropical heat stroke.
paced stepped brisk new york city in february
smacked in face by your brisker maternal open
fist backhand wake up call.
five more minutes mom!
the way you carry chicago fourth of july
fireflies
and your ability to propel the smell of the
seasoned hot dogs to my nose blows my mind.
pickle on the side. no mustard gas please.
the way you carry airplanes the same way
through airways battleships waterways
effortlessly. fly is to take off and land and to
float is to withstand the beginning or the end.

i dream of flying, but if i'm already the vehicle
traveling at speeds of sound best friended by the
birds and bees how much farther do i have to go
you ask? the speed of light.
all i want to do is float in you
with you.

fire.

i take most cues from you

necessary masculine dangerous
flames dance femme blue blood red skin

procured light
produced to keep the darkness away
don't get too close.
you are transformative by design
impurities consumed by engulfment
purified in ways we may not understand
i can try
but as soon as i stare in your eyes mine swell
tears cry hypnotized by your rarified spiritual
knowledge of the divine.
you appear from the sky shot zig zagged
or i create you from energy combusted,
feed you to keep you alive,
fire placed in fireplace to keep warm,
watch you grow and shrink in size
then with one swift wind or washed wave watch
you disappear with smoked goodbyes
and from what's left

the burning ashes embered i remember
one day, with the perfect love crashed
once again you will rise
you are alchemy
pure

wood.

you sprout from seed
photosynthetically
branch out
species make home in your soul

feed from your fruit

you're cut
chopped
pieces torn apart
utilized used by without consent
logs built and bought paper
receipted in your flesh and blood

you make homes
art hand carved
and your fire fuels it

from your fruits
every fiber of your trees
respected
we feed

metal.

before you were head bangers
we banged heads in attempt to
differentiate all ninety-one of you
periodically shifting
malleable without breakage

shape shifting
shielding protective
fusible fusing when attracted
magnetic attraction
drawn out and drawn out and drawn thin
ductile, all while baring strength
within.

you are precious.

so precious i'll risk losing you, well thrown,
just to make a wish.

light.

encircle me in your white double deed vitaminic
electromagnetic wavelengths of universal love
and divinic protection

bask
from sun to flame to chandelier
the way you shine on,
remind me why i'm here,
show me
where i'm going

and from all darkness
comes you
as it is always born from within

energy.

i'd rather have a bundle of you
water wind and sun

than keep creating waste of you,
from you,
combustion

what is your potential?
kinetically speaking
dance not for me
but with me
that is electricity

your only negative aspect is the human that
chooses to manipulate your frequencies

everything on a nuclear level is you
all of it is moved
in all directions
by you

i am positive
in your vitalitics abilities
a ball of you floating through space
infinitely

east.

cock a doodle do i realize you are the one that
wakes me?
bakes me in your glories?
good morning baby.

as i look to you i bow my head for your offerings
are consistent. timely, to rid me of this
darkness and add light to
the ever glowing ever growing
light within. without hesitation, your rise of
grand sun grants hope, granted. a new day is cast
upon us. i look to you to shine light on
yesterday's hardships and allow me the courage
to take on whatever may come, for this day is
special. this day is the only day i have. it is
because of you that all things begin. i am
calling on all spirits of your direction
to help guide me in today's journey.
fill me with enough
imagination willpower and mental clarity to
tackle any form of fear that shall arise for i
know no matter what, we will rise again.

let there be light

south.

now listen here y'all. no matter where i stand i
know beneath me stands you and i am forever
grateful for your strength to hold me up. when
they say that heat rises i know they're talking
round you. warm is warm is warm is warm and
i'm warmer in your home brew. under my toes
grow roots that connect us all someway
somehow. i feel less individual because of you
and however crazy this may sound i'm grateful
for your qualities unifying. flying low are your
fertile grounds that ground me home and if home
is where the heart is, i love knowing that i am
southern to somewhere no matter what. i call to
all spirits of your direction to give me courage
to continue to water my seeds planted and watch
them grow sprouted in your soil. flourish from
action as all things need tending to. nurture my
lands singing hymns to plants as when i grow in
size, my heart does too, and so do you.

west.

may my wild wild ways bid adieus as i face you
for all that has been will sail way as night
falls i fall with you. what goes up must come down to
rest. as the sun sets in your direction i shall
set intentions for this hibernation. prayers and
meditations. teach me in this night sleep all
that is sounded has the chance to be silenced for in
this eve i dream from you. heal baby heal. dear
you, may i be granted this wish of astral travel
and grace me with gifts of my own subconscious
in order to awaken the conscious. bon voyage
through this mirage of fantasy and whatever
nightmare may stare me down scared, know i am
student to your teachings. i call to all spirit
leaders of your direction and ask for sweet
lullabies as your ancestral souls tuck me in for
this dormancy. remind me of stories of creation
and evolution as i evolve more into the one i was
always destined to be. replenish from your
calming seas and as rain falls from your ways i
beg on knees wash all my earthly sins away.
stillness in this womb as i regenerate rejuvenate
for tomorrow is new, and soon will be day. for
all that is wild and unknown is just a trek
through space. now rested. more prepared

north.

you the star of the show as whenever i'm lost,
look up to show up, you guide me home. as the
wisest of directional protectors, i raise my head
to gaze upon your subtle grand bodied ways as
your luminescent spirit never fades. as above so
below i pray this primary goal fixed shall not
waive till this body pass away and my spirit's
ascensions meet to yours light in heaven. i call
on your directional elders, shamanic storytellers
epic, to penetrate my intellect intelligently
for my design intelligently inspired by yours divine.
up your way is colder and when the seasons
change to winter one year older my body shivers
as your wind stirs reminding me i am still alive.
winter always is coming and as beautifying and
mystic your white sheets cover soil i call on you
for protection to withstand blizzardy frosted
bites coil. i ask for your rays of wisdom to come
down and change ways, transform the greens to
grays as in this gray space i know that all color
will show and grow again.

twinkle
twinkle
how i wonder
taught by you
shining bright no matter what

time.

watch out.
for a second imagine your history
sun-water-sand-candle-pendulum-bells-gravity-
springs-electricity-atomic
this very minute
continually in process, progress
around the clock we clock
this progression
our hours dwindling,
the hours everlasting
not on my watch
twenty-four cycles
fixed lifetimes
not born yesterday
may die tomorrow
what do i know?

i know i watch you as to measure
accomplishments and setbacks past present and
future marked recognizable.
i know my internal clock tells you better than my
iphone

i just wish i had more of you to love
all the you in the world.

all of it is you all of it is you all
of it is you. (third yous the charm)

calendar.

since the beginning of time, it's been said,
all life has been scheduled. tracked by stars.

leaping

today the most commonly used map of time is
structured off the birth and death of one man.

jesus.

matrix.

do i take the
blue pill
or
the red pill?

i take both.

tap in
to
tap out

side effects
may include
two thousand seventeen.

shadow.

your size
dependent on time
a life requires
light
as does mine

a friendly reminder; the dark is always lurking,
made in your image
you have the power to create it and from it grow.

whether or not choose to cast you in this
blockbuster,
darling, you should win an oscar for that
performance.

crystal.

beautiful, multi-faceted conduit
of wizardry, pure
though not always clear
on which of you do what,
still,
rock headed,
backpack always heavier
collector
of energies
new age
pseudoscientific
practitioner
charged moon sun salted

mine spherical
as prefer your edges smooth

i sometimes dream of swallowing you
popping pills of all your kinds
crushing your crystalline structures
cutting lines with tarot cards
blowing rails of your prismatic flesh
suppose that's just the junkie in me
and there's a crystal for that

spring.

as you breathe this new life,
i promise to do the same.

awakening the you in my step
as sprung chrysanthemum garland fields
yield growth once again reborn chance to dance
in poppies crop topped
stop to smell the roses begin again
poses for photos as the grass turns green
the bird's song sing
the bees pollinate floral beds clean
aurora sheens seen skin glisten as rain showered
cry tears joyed as this resurrection is always
miracled no matter third day
every friday is a good one once you've arrived.
i am not your chicken yet still find joy in not
hunting rather now hiding your coin and cash
filled eggs as that's how things are done in my
family italian
passover the joys full of you for the fore season
was the harsh one and you reminding that all will
too soon
bloom again.
revel in this revivified awakening

summer.

wet hot ultraviolet sunsets like burning grass
cigarettes slow churned butter lettuce honey
mustard vinaigrette
you are stupendous
mid solstice blasts days open nights shortest,
leaves room to wander longer at waters sanded
crest to search for gold.
one swallow doesn't make you
but a shotgunned chug on the fourth makes it
closer.
fire worked celebratory as your temperatures
scorch this fire works independently
for my blood typed warm blooded as born from
mother gutted at the end of july.
worth this heat as your months are for goonies
treating all seven days as holidays.
not a vacation without some adventure air
conditioning and the stench of saltwater close.
some people say your birthdays the worst but i
prefer being alone on my days of birth so i was
happy school was out for you and me
still am.
this is our time
it's our time
down here
i'd say i'd die for you, but goonies never say die

fall.

the only season with two names
reason as autumn came first,
after your leaves fall.
fresh breath of fresher air staring at fauna and
flora spectrums shift clear for you are the
second coming of spring but instead of flowers
blossoming your leaves transform colored shift
gears pre-tree toss 'em.
automatic exhale.
autumn chanting om.
inhale that honey crisp orchard fog.
raking loaves of leaves midwestern home
can smell the fifty degrees haze stewing of your
piles fallen bones as leap
to fall to fall to fall to fall
knowing your golden arms will catch me.

melancholia flown.

winter.

winter.

holy days seasoned bleached
snow white salted streets
everything elsa frozen.
frosty frosted windshields icicled rude off red
nosed bitter cold. your solstice. as days get
shorter evenings push longer stronger winds
blow caps and stems lose leaves.
i've lived in cities where you don't visit and
thought for a while preferred my time away from
you until i moved back to new york and realized
our long-distance relationship wasn't working
for me west coasted.
see, i need you.
as much as i dread your blizzard days in april
trekking to subways layered in god knows what
god whistling air that freezes as walked i'm
reminded of the cycle that god blows. one two
three four. and after the fourth back to one.
you are the rest before the awakening and even
though sensitive to your chilling nature, it's
codependent and love our extremes.
you me a beanie and a fireplace baby, that's all
we need.

gravity.

you are indeed special
nature's first law
but not that special
in that all laws are meant to break

go up
to
always come down
yes,
only for next time
to go higher

no need to chase the dragon if the dragon is
where it begins.

fly baby, fly
you will never keep us down

rainbow.

after cleansing weep,
you remind me
from all storm comes
light,
rowed.
spectrum spectacular
no one's color of more importance.
all created equal
pots of gold,
and that's all us
other
flag folk are fighting for.

roy g. biv for president

plant.

from seed to feed speak to me.
whisper sweet nothings in ears truest
all-knowing calls as vines never lie
nor treat liars.
cover me shaded. expansionary higher.
in your amazon king of jungles where more than
half of you wake beyond amazing.
amazonian neck deep pulmonary pump in carbon
deeds out oxygen bleeds. color me colored
lively color as all born from you.
dense greens. primal homes day hunt
night sleep. herbal remedies medicinal natural
however, you have been known to poison so be
sure to know whose of your berries get picked.
sickness cured or sickness endured as some for
you some for me. the beginning of life's cycle
stemmed blend and ground in roots below of life
you tree of life.
we may not have grown from you but grow with
you tandem. walls talk wisest listen.
i wonder if your feelings get hurt when eaten raw
or cooked or if that's the whole point of your
sprouts edible eligibility.
consume the vegetables moss algae fungus
seaweed grains nuts legumes roots and fruits of
your labor, your growth, for us to grow more.
sprouting mind body spirit.
your based diet people question where proteins
get fed but always remember gorillas are
vegetarian.
i respect you, a student to your teachings.
i bow my head to you gratitude.
now let me get a kale avocado salad please.

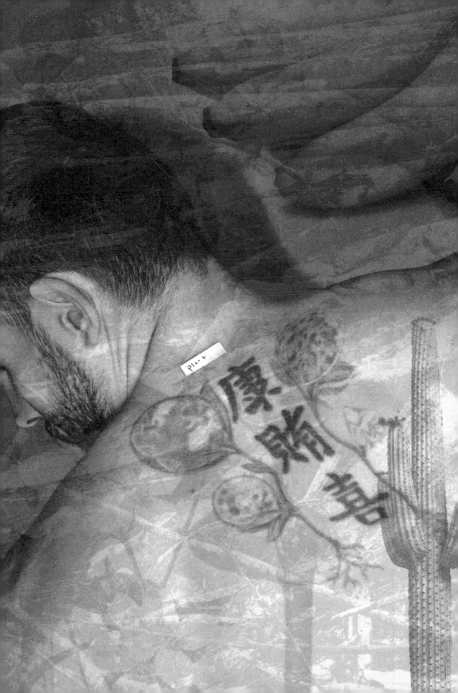

animal.

kingdom so vast and today my plane rather small
it would be impossible to do justice covering
your spirit lands in just one trip. so, must this
just be about a dog named sun.
all of it is you baby girl.
i have a chihuahua named sun that was gifted to
me two years young two and half pound runt that
is as much a part of me as my right foot, but
smaller. she speaks a love language i've never
dreamed. walking down street sight peculiar. i
stand as six-foot man she a six-inch blonde with
a furry prance almost obscene.
this little creature tiny has taught me more
unconditional than any. see when people see her
they smile, gleam automatically. more like her
we should all aspire to be.
in love with the way you snort when you need
something or just when your smelly ass breathe
breathes. in love with your bug eyes looking for
spots between my legs to sleep and outside to
squat pee. i love the way you want to be held all
day and you don't even realize you're the one
really doing the holding.
sun you are my everything. i the father to your
sun, and you the sun to my land and dad's coming
home soon, i promise.

continent.

pangea split
one for each day of the week
monday being antartica
one for each color of the rainbow
north america seems orange
contained
main land masses
obsolete
imagine if it was you
that wore the flag,
how much simpler things would be
or how
much more difficult.
remember we all came from one.

country.

one hundred and ninety-five of you
and
not one shithole.

america.

oh, say can you see
all fifty not so united states
and shades of gray between texas red and now
alabama blue? god shed his grace amazing grace
in your cities crayola melted pots where streets
paved golden to royal lakes great top of white
mountain ranges of greens and nudes. grand
canyon's yellows reds and orange potions
voodoo from salem to new orleans to
native cultured god bless you this land is your
land, always has been, forever will

the black out of puerto rico are you, america,
afraid of the dark or just unwilling to help?

red white and blue proven to do and be to
breathe above sea level. but just like me these
colors sometimes these colors run and stars once
tall empires fall they cheat. the land of sort of
mostly free. deconstructed. up to us to put the
pieces back together.
underneath it all, heart still alive.
as are you my sweets,
as vile as you may sometimes seem.
you grew me.
i love you.
no matter what.

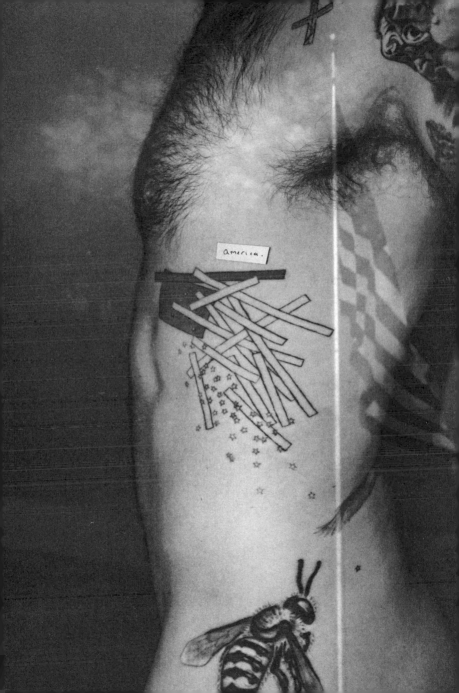

america.

city.

bright lights big you
don't need you
but
want you.
sometimes.
as i
can't seem
to get away from this urban jungled feeding.
as some dreams will die
for some made.

ocean.

respect your power
have faith waved,
dive in your deep
unknown to hit floors.
shores for born
message carried.
i just don't care for
your sanded grit,
but sacrifice as to
get lost in it.

mountain.

want to climb
every foot by foot by foot
ascending to your peak
just to see the view
for you are worth it

moved by you
so
i can move you.

plains.

great horizoned skies
prairies in all directions
no end in sight.

and nothing
can ever
get in our way.

desert.

bare boned sander dunes
rays blasted
casted constant
makes you,
mirage.
for in your abysses
dryness vast
well a well a well
is treasure
to find,
myself.

forest.

merrily skip
over rivers of flossed moss
and through your
canopied enchantress
wilderness
to reunite with all the
pixie wizard troll witchy sorcerers
wolf and robin hooded boy girl twin fairy tales
that live
inside
me.

arctic.

glide in your
frigid whiteness
clear minded to
remind this boy
no matter how frozen
time seems,
coy,
all iciness one day
inevitably
begins to melt.

home.

your comforted nest
resides not in
where i live
but
in how i feel.

and baby,
i feel you.

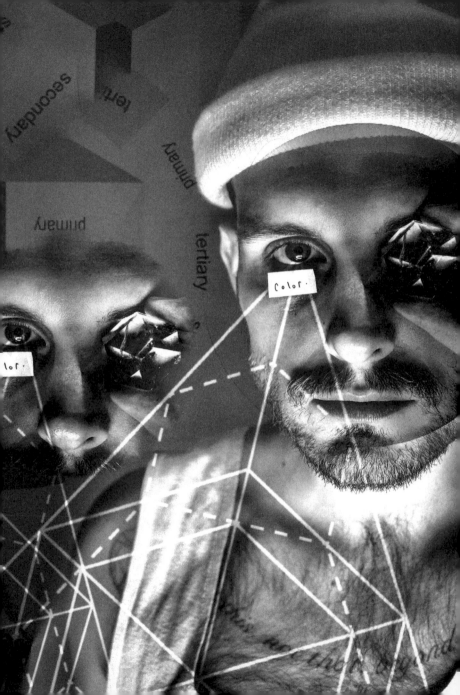

color.

this is a story
about a girl
with magic eyes

see, we
have three cones
to
pick you up
draw you in
wheeled.

she has four.

apparently,
she can see
ninety-nine million more
of you
and i don't know what to do
with this information
of your increased population.

really
how much more beautiful can you all get?

this story is true.

tool.

ingenuity
discover pathways to
make easier
or
more difficult
as
intention matters

from palo santo
gut cleansed
to skill saw
cut edged
as skills saw light
used

screw the ill mannered,
gut wrenched

possession.

you are not
in
what i carry;
lift up.

but in what carries me;
lifted.

community.

village it takes
meant to build
webbed
yin to yang to yin to yang
power not just in numbers but in its
distribution.
frequencies supported.

we are not all
members of different tribes,
just
different beliefs.
and that's ok.

money.

only earn
if
made you
in love

richest.

weapon.

most dangerous in the world;
the human that does not love oneself.

most powerful, the greatest;
the one that does.

war.

wonder
how many more
need fighting
need to die
for us to realize
anymore not needed

the only battlefield
we should be proud
to stand ground
is within ourselves.

religion.

did god create man or man create gods and if
gods created man what created god?

more than forty-two hundred faiths
and creeds
public systems cultural
sacred private
faith exposable
sharable beliefs
cosmically knowable
rebuilding potentially
epically destructible

the only one
on to something
is the one
heartedly whole
believed

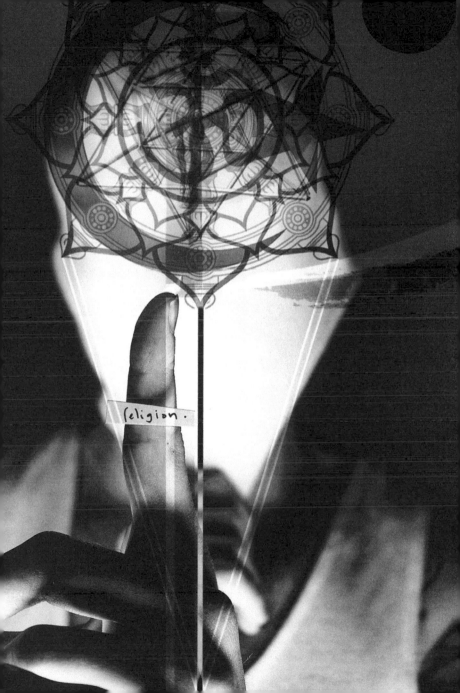

science.

evolution of knowledge
based in your
(for now)
relative facts.

i just wish we could love you without always
looking for something more.

politics.

the
greatest
show
on
earth

lives on

law.

rules set in place
temporary
like sandcastles
built awaiting wakes
understand thy terrain
and plan accordingly
for breaks
reliant
on thine
judge alone
calls all bodies home
so
you be the judge

prison.

beyond the locked caged bars steel
beyond the nine million behind
beyond the outweighed collegiate campus
beyond the nonviolent drug offenses
beyond the profiling racial
beyond the taxpaying cost
beyond the act smarter sentencing
live the everyday locked up
imprisoned
held captive by minds thoughts fears
fear not
for the skeleton key swallowed jailbreaks for
gives free
forgiveness in inners near

forgive yourself first
as to doors popped unlock
bailed release

spirituality.

i clear space
for you
as to fall down
rabbit holes
as once you know
the real work begins

the practice of
self-care

spirit ritual
rituality's duality
masculinity femininity
triangle up to triangle down
merkaba bodies merkabodied
in love

fall in love
with the practice
of yourselves.

internet.

part of the last generation
to know
what life was like
before you

inner net safetied stronger
knowing anything minds desired
accessible with the
click clickity click clack click clack smack click
space back click search
boom
mind blown

living breathing
global consciousness
for free

hopefully it stays that way
(prayers for net neutrality)

music.

dancing through wind remedied
you and me
air to ear dynamic

a song first heard carries power
fact is dynamism
at minimum, listeners you engage
feel feels certain ways
away pain washed washes away
the new song's weight
dynamite waiting to pop blaze
momentarily forget scape

songs remembered hold memory of time to
place
you remind me of one
space between notes filled won
treble body trembled bass
days triggers moments linger
put fingers on needing you like rhythm needs
melody needs harmony needs beat instrumental
to a cappella spoken toned in sung song speaks

nce nce nce nce nce nce nce nce nce nce
one good thing one good thing one good thing
about you;

we are you
waiting and willing
press play

art.

(this page is empty for you, as all great
needs canvas blank space. create.)

film.

something happened
to someone
something sometime
worthy of record
visual recorded

every time
screens powered up
big to small fiction to non
a piece of you
is born again
viewer mirrored roll mirrors roles

powers down to do something with it

that something happened
happens
to me

technology.

discipline applied practically
consume ripened pre-rot
as all shelf life
temporary
relative to its user
even the wheel reinvented
(look it up)

you pull us apart to
bring us together
to pull us apart to bring us together
roundabouted but remember without us you
disappear.

performance.

easy for me to
wear the masks to mask masked
out of insecurity
imitation flatters
when though
i
wear myself
per form my own man
confidant
realest pure
confidents
wins the gold statue
awarded
as i become one

literature.

time travel
tangible real
because of you written.

pick up a book and go somewhere.

numbers.

0123456789

oh universal magic coded
with your lines, straight
curved silky smooth
definite truths
unite us
as
counting on you

39.

history.

lessons unfolding over centuries
egos, sword, tempers, guns
lectures taught in lives lost
education systemic for those
it benefits

for a better world
most perceptive learnt
how to be more than
what not to do

the wake is now
the rest is you

dare not be on the wrong side
every day we're making new
no need to rewrite
when
written right

angels.

just wing it
for
it could happen.

place of worship.

knock knock on doors
who's their god where spirt abodes
take me to church temple synagogue monastery
mosque shul shrine cathedral
holy places natural destinations tabernacle on
sterling saddles
venerate reverence devote
venerate reverence devote who
are the ones that worship more
architecture's highest arted form
as source, direct from source
for us so to simply sit bow kneel a while
contemplate
light a candle on my altar
give thanks
pray for change
always open somewhere to
he she them their arms wide
he she them always there
waiting on us to
knock knock on doors

god.

all of it
on earth
is you

universe.

big bang.

everything
from nothingness
antimatter you mattered matter
prehistoric fireball
dense explosion cosmic flow it
times beginnings took flight to scramble sound
if a star born to fall shoot universal
could you be heard if no one to listen?
or were they listening to each other
vast talk smack
fat whack
chock full slam
super mondo clack
creationism theorized einstein
yet i have time hard heads wrapping
from nothing spurs something
even twenty billion years ago
for you were always something to begin, and
that's enough for me.

and from something comes everything.

more than the beginning,
you the reminder that all life's capable
just waiting on the button pressed
as within pulsates expansive
drumfire boom rumble
detonate
to constantly expand.

space.

between you and me
relative stance guided
spatial wided
the physicality
between you and me
your cadet is the one that will fly
between you and me
more yours
less mine
however shared
as in you we take up hand to hand
your existence need not me
on the other hand
honey to be
i need you.

solar system.

lover
you are the sun
plus
everything
that orbits
about it

astronomy.

you
keep
me
always
wanting
to
look up.

sun.

they may say your sized average,
aged middling, considering galaxies
as you are just one star among billions
else they say you're not a planet.
how than are you my ruler?
well,
i say they're erring fluffed
as you're balled giant, vitaminic pyre,
coursed diurnally, dawning day
wages on all time bodies space

for you rise to set burn for us to
heal to grow to prune
shed as all things need shed light shines on
mind's eye mines i
love you no matter if i can't see you
for i know someone on the other side can
needs to.

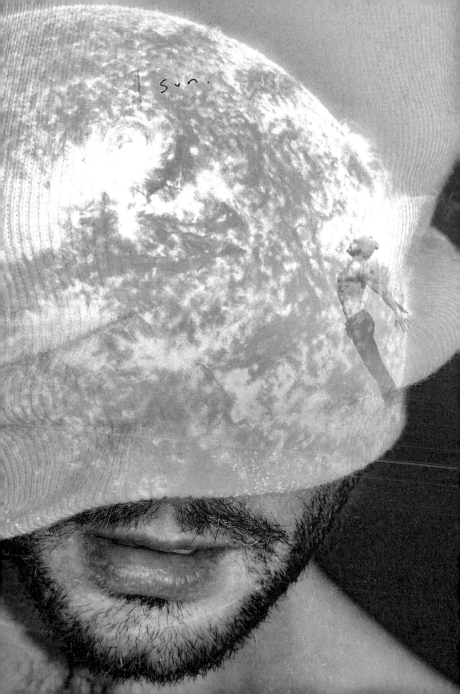

moon.

phased by you directly
selenophile direct face to face
cycles land new to full
heavens altar candle wax to wane about
crescent pleasant gibbous give me this
to die out dark side shadow turn around
fluorescent white impregnate
to gain a new perspective start
anew waves move wave goodnight to
evening cratered swiss firmament
holy i love you

to you and back i mean meant no matter what a
time to shine
promise me if i promise you i will
bark at you howl now
ahhhooooooooooooooooowhoo
ask for you even though don't have to
reach for you beg
bleed red for you
cry for you weep
i'll ever never be over you
they say there's a man on sided well
if he's anything like me i understand
hell, he just can't stay away
for even in the darkest of time
you my love shine on
show the way
for if you can change so can we

stars.

what does it take to be one of you?
if i'm already made not of your dust
ratherish your light
sidereal its real
shoot make a wish
some folk need you carved to boulevard
i'm happy with your twinkle twinkles
in eyes
carved to skies
(for now)

mercury.

talk to me in whispers.
mister be sure not to slip poison tongues
tell me your secrets
blistered bleak landscape
second smallest in size packs powerful punch
days long years short only eighty-eight plays
around father's rays.
mercurius, named by romans' god messenger
with feathers winged sandals ankled for went
and came and as messages still arrive
are you the one to blame for zeitgeisted
retrogrades ways? never sign a contract in your
backways technologic betrays logic dismays
though time for all re's praise.
let me rephrase, babe,
please communicate the words of gods
brains amorphous
to palpable ear waves directly
as i rely on your steadfastness speedy gonzales
full thoughtfulness focused amazed
planetary ballet.

venus.

seduce me enchanted
as i landed on your glittered jewel
supple sexed up desired
love goddess of touch my skin caress with lips
your hot dry sweetness to wet this
as i honor your bodies danced rotation slow, take
your time to spin ladybird as i take all of it in
one day on you lasts more than a year
though i could spend a lifetime getting lost in
your orbit breath flowed, hair curled cult
femme tell me where
where and when the next gathering is set
devotional to your planetary celestine feminine
prophecy motion.
they say you're a sister to my home
though couldn't be more different
as most sisters are opposite,
just a phone call away
can you have your sister give me your number
so i can send you sonnets written on your fervor
curves inked blood sweat and come maybe one
day you and me could meet in person and fall
further.

mars.

red god, take me with you
to war strap on golden armored chest plates
and lets you and me face it feathered helmet
head on action is the force energized by your
surprise attacks
don't act surprised
as i masc for masc for your masculine wins
battles fought not just to defeat the parts of me
ready to kill
will you tell me of your lands seized sized half
of mines candy apple covered crated desolate
barren caring?
of your mile-high volcano and who it shoots for
or who its blarings shoot at?
sir warrior man, can you tell me why sometimes
i'm angry and how i express it however
indirectly suppressed malefic?
initiate me in your crimson passion ways
instigated actions based only by your lessoned
crusade on which are worthiest of fighting for
just promise to take me with you
to protect you as you protect me.
for life on you exists in we.

jupiter.

allow me to serve you holiest of thou holy king
of all king's god of all jove
show me what it means to rule
bolt thundered soared eagle regal
throne in space holds massive weight largest of
all marbled round thirteen hundred times mine
brightest in skies after suns and venus
as your jewelry, royal shines twice as bright as
the casted sunlight it strikes for all to see
sixteen moons orbit more pull as king you are
optimistic in your quickness living day ten-hour
specific expansiveness as you blast candidness to
fathom this life is worth living aware cared for
by your rule of thumb
the greater benefic gets done however
bless me with all ten fingers
and i promise to serve you properly humbled by
thou great one
as to rule
one day ruler
becomes

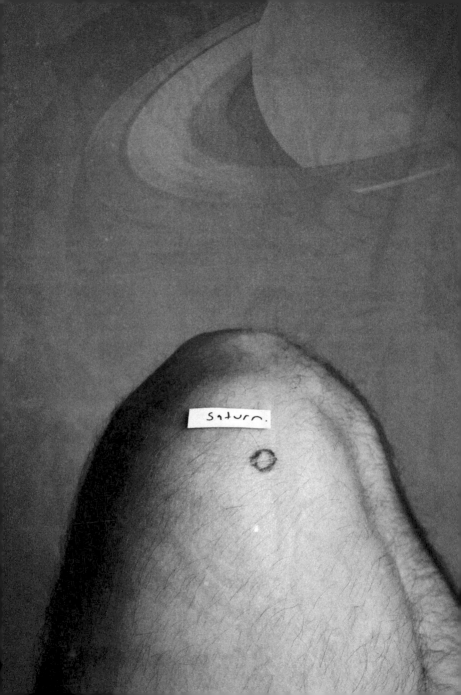

saturn.

excuse me sir can you tell me the time of which
your abundance becomes mine?
is it in your return at twenty-eight
lord of rings spin
as matter not yet known pre or post moon
eighteen of those known titan flown though
space mass weight less than water as if you fell
in oceans you'd float saunter as boat boasts
gaseous flash this liberation your golden age in
history as wealthy peace and plenty of ways to
see past limits and boundaries set healthy
crystallizations of sickles in hand as
agricultured lands materialize plans on saturdays
born from yours name similar to satan's but
that's for a different time and place experience
gained when you show me schedules disciplined as
to make me the man i've always dreamt of
excuse me sir can you tell me
the time is now.

uranus.

tell me a joke that's not a play on names
words as youth learn of your epithetic label
rather fables of your pale greens,
mated with gaia, father of our blue skies
earth size four times than hers, ring less
seen others tell me
of your rebellious awakenings
surprise me with tales of validity
radical risks taken
as you sail sideways with fists shaken
heavens personification, god of all the planets
you are the funniest not for puns farce tricked
rather ways you pick me up shocked
to reveal how i will react this day and age
fact crazed
will be the man that holds onto the past
rather accepting lessons
breath of refreshes air to breakthrough
forgive me though
for no matter what
lol
by named you

neptune.

sing me a song to the tune of waves
crashed by your brass
three-pronged trident
breathe fresh waters daughter
made mermaid voice way clear
hypnotize me space deep to subconscious
as dreams flaunt this
you're far more remote
far aways dream sleep nights
creep crashed fierecest winds sweep
blue seas seen spirituality
prayers and meditations
i believe in you and me
reap benefits of fantasies calming this reality
briny as to earn one's keep
hush baby melodied lullabies
god of water thus god of tears
cried egos lie
sing me a song father
as i go to sleep in your waters
deaf to nothing but the hymns of hims
to remind me that from oceans i came and from
source you came as to all
in all it all goes back to beginnings
sing me a song father
sing me a song

pluto.

show me the underworld lord almighty
in spite of what's in store
whether it be purgatory hellish
or harvest bountiful wealth
mouthful well wishes of seeds
waiting to sprout glory be thy dark sided
name dwarfed goofy discovered only in nineteen
thirty since then shed status planetary
and i'm sorry for the heart splitting breakup
i'm sure it wasn't you, it's us i suppose
the longest distance relationship finally
abducted like proserpina, like hiroshima
dropped bombs away
with the shadows to make way for light
shines on you dim as moonlight your moon
charon
orbits skewed who are you really
if not the one farthest away knew god knows
there's always something farther new
transform me
newer as i die buried six feet from my flesh
grows reborn
new just promise me you won't tell me what to do
as i've always had a problem with authority

astrology.

there was a time
once upon
when your zodiac
body language celestial
bestial worshipped religious
in mass
now sublanguage scientific pseudo
back of the newspaper
though still notes held tenuto
by those who know how to sing
your signs point
is to the one waited for.

you keep me always wanting to just look up to
look in as below so above.

those times are coming back
happily ever after

aries.

first out the gate ram race take flight
not to be confused with god of war
although you have been known to battle stubborn
like my brother deepest lover
chaotic aggression wearing scars on hearts
forever picking scabs to bleed
for golden fleece bandaged blanketed
life's hitch only what you make of it
signed fire cardinal natural born red
though as the color represents to love loyalist
or to burn spoil
it's you always on one side of fence
there is no in between
you are either the best
or
you are the worst
though deep down i know, not either
have anything to do with me.

taurus.

second
the bull of heaven and hell sustained by lack of
change commitment craves for you love to be
love to beloved even with your poker face steer
cautious this way even with expiration dates
sexploration tastes sensual
down to earth signed earth kind
never ones to fly away for nest is home even for
the ones known
with horns to think harder
wished you didn't feel you had to hide tears with
fears of being seen
vulnerable
even though i love you for not telling me you
love me until you mean it,
then it will probably be
too bold for me to keep it.

gemini.

third
oh, the gem in my eye eyes immortalized
twins castor and pollux hand in hand
papa zeus united them together in heavens this is
normalized on earth
as me and you united here as well
the love of my life is one of you
inevitably airs ways and means
there are more than one, multiples
which is the greatest type of love
as monotony at no time crops up
close-up to far exceeds expressiveness
alive to lively liven scenes whimsical
quick à la whip tip toe knows show
me the sides you can't public reveal
as you my dear are multidimensional
flexible and even when tensional whine ass
pissed
i love you for it
as always,
no matter what
twin flips

cancer.

fourth
your name ears violate rather
spirit high elated not just the abscess wriggling
figuring giant shellfish clawed crab chief of
water signs ruled by moon's tides
so brain fluid flow
sections introspective enigmatic empathic you
feel like my best friend
clairvoyant yet may not know it
means you're just more in touch with touch
sensation and feelings that i love the way you
listen to me understand the way i believe
now how can i help you listen
understand better see yourself?

leo.

fifth
rarr.
king of beasts spar nemean lion impenetrable
hide not from fire as born from it sun ruled ray
rey of the jungle
i fathered in your dates with stars july thirtieth
mythological fly as constellation maps manes
main flirtatious can look but dangerous to touch
me with your paws bold heart of golden creative
created and prepared to explode if need be
protective of your cave and pack slave
back and forth for your lioness get this center
of attention but be careful not to seem arrogant
as your glorious nature can seem flagrant to those
less blatant in their fur.
i am in love with you because duh i am you and
that's what wildcats do.

leo.

virgo.

sixth
like a virgin
as the final immortal deserted earth
touched heaven for the very first time
maiden made in stars
meticulously placed as fates knows perfections
face impeccable taste straight white silk laced
with philanthropic service, you serve it on
sterling silver plates
humble overachieving love is the ultimate
reward however independent you may seem as
the virgin dreams to lose it every once in a
while it's been since you let me read your emotions
seem calculated though i love you for trying
to be perfect even with the insight that
perfectionism exists
just the way you are.

libra.

seventh
the only one of twelve symbolized inanimate
though your scales mechanical
weighing and outweighing
divine law and custom for you themis to lady
justice justified in your grace and fairness as
balance acts
what the library held read a book just to keep up
with your beauty
deeper than skin deep thoughts logic based
although spirituality creates om freedom from
your own creed abilities to always see both sides
as scaled play stories of right and wrong and
there's nothing wrong with walking miles in all
the shoes
how else would you babe know what to do.
i am madly in love with you as my rising sign
glued to your brass register and from my feline
sun's blaze you are just what i need to create
real change.
blessed in your air.

scorpio.

eighth
scorpion sent to slay orion
for he was trying to obliterate all life on earth
and won eternal spirit
ethereal story real or not you headed hot
determined to thrive not just underworld rather
transform new above grounded in shedding light
on nights all right passion
zealous jealous feeling intense
magnetized prized abilities to draw in and
outside the lines being eyes seeing past the box
straight to soul knows more if you can let some
of yourself out for me to see. redheaded fury
scurries like waves as water taught her fire
sometimes vapor creates. i love you eight legged
arachnids for you have more legs to stand on
than most with dexterity to sting spit roast.

sagittarius.

ninth
half man half horse centaur chiron fire on arrow
bowed archer bow blunt savage arch pulled
pointed to scorpius's chest should they not know
best life has to offer the grandest expeditions
or else shoot straightest as of sarcasm latest even
though you keep it realest what they see is what
they get wisdom as immortal student hunting
takes knowing noticing even the basal of detail i
love you for real always on the prowl for
enlightened ideas even if you have a hard time
savoring the kill.

capricorn.

tenth
half goat half fish one horned of cornucopia one
swims through saltwater
cronus father of deities had five kids though
eated these to himself keep safe
earth captain happens ruled by saturn
mountain goat ascends slow steady round bends
for nothing to reach your top goal scored success
heap of class act determined to climb
even the tallest of ladders
reach for heavens though times more flexible can
be you with directions to the nearest detour as
failing is not an option rather lesson
i love you like my ex-boyfriend as you are
always the funniest one in rooms
and i'm sorry
for ever hurting you as i may never understand
fully you but consistently mine minds blow
blew.

aquarius.

eleventh
ganymede bared water on earth made cup
bearer by jupiter king of gods to gods
though air signed and ruled by saturn
the duality from fluid to wind keeps the rivers
flowing as all you are is flow progressive in the
age of you can change for goods greater
rebellion in instigating effects visionary
pursuits inspiration blooms from your lakes make me
want to be better though together you and me are
joined in stars as with my first breath the moon
suckled your breast laid deep in nooked chest
and i am crazy about you for making me crazy
god i love your fluid blaze even if you send me
to confused and dazed from you comes all great
space grandiose creates

pisces.

twelfth
one fish aphrodite two fish eros transmuted as to
escape paddle waters from typhon's ways
constellations oldest date in your ancient age
christ born space ruled by neptune holds stories
of scaled ways you interact today emotional in
you where all real magic lay mermaid souls as
deep seated as oceans crazed craved you be
mystic spiritual fix this imbalance of reality to
fantastical maze through your eyes as heavy as
shine bright my diamond for i love the way you
see me take free to stroke butterfly through
heavens and i promise to try and keep you
grounded as magicians great always need one
hand to sky and one to planet we founded earth

galaxy.

you
pull
it
together
all
matter
what

milky way.

i've got the golden ticket
and
as much as i love the taste of your rivers milked
drips
you are all but one confectionary
in this willy wonkad chocolate factory
and i tooth sweet

nico tortorella

sirius.

pinky swears
serious
a star
never
shined so bright
as when you
my dear
are near

orion.

oh, mighty hunter man
sometimes i wonder
which direction your shield and club stand facing
and
whether or not your belts
cinched wasted
divine design pyramid created
something worth celebrating
your swords nursery nebulae creating millions of
new stars born
or
if you're just another man with a weapon being
chased by none other than a scorpio ready to fight
because you have to.

north star.

how many poems have been
written emo lyrics
songs scream singed
nautical stars tattooed
on chest stretched shoulder to shoulder for you
to know we care
to follow your point
me to the right direction home
as my real household
is closer to polaris than this
stranger terrace i'm leaning over
neck cranked
with just a hand rolled
just to stare known
fixed by fixed
northern you

dippers.

the first constellation
i ever remember
learning of
big and little
cuddled
sixty-nine miles per hour
team huddled
captain star north
chicago bears
hers a major
hers a minor
ladled to scoop
baptized by night sky's poured stars over faces
mine as gods pound
truth cries

asteroid.

i've heard it said
that it was your kind
that wiped out
the dinosaurs
the kind that orbit space
shaped irregular
chunks of matter of fact
mineral rich
that never came together
to form planet
but i've also heard it said
what if
you were the flying object
unidentified
that delivered
the aliens
us
that took this planet
from them
to call it
our own

well, shit

meteor.

the only time
it's safe to say
i hope you burn
before we
get a chance
to properly meet
the only time
i'd rather
stand outside your showers
to watch falls
rather than
clean

nebula.

collapse for me
blast skies like aurora borealis
get lost in your indirect fog hazed
set wallpapers by quotes inspirational
as from your effervescent catastrophe
illume cataclysmic annihilation
the pillars of all creation
erect palatial
and from that silent walloped bang
a star is born
collapse for me baby
collapse for me

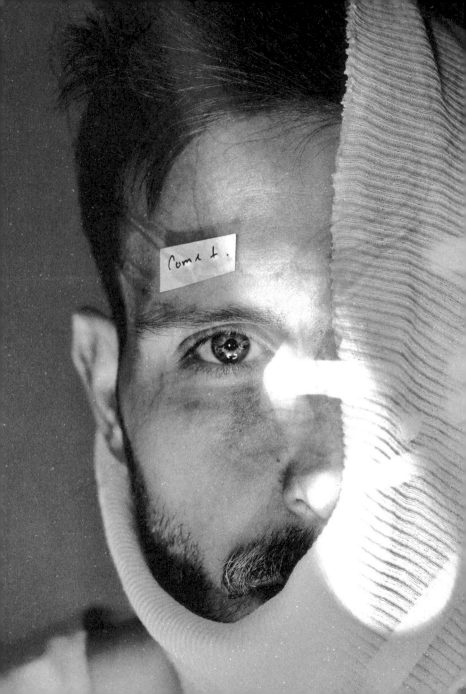

comet.

filthy snowballs just like us
traveling dust collected falls starlike
omens of souls returning
shoots through skies fly stupid
blamed outbreaks of plagues
sleigh mate of cupid
now dasher now prancer
now coma from fiery lips
sayonara

the only way to see you
is to catch you by the tail
before it's too late

black hole.

let's be honest
a hole's a hole
even yours however unknown
infinitely leading
to nowhere
and
once one goes black
time and space altogether stop
they never go back

spacejunk.

curious more than what happens
to all the satellites used
since nineteen fifty-seven
other man-made technologies
that are of use no longer
the ones yet to shoot
the you in the hundreds of thousands
not counting your bits of debris
whipping round twenty-five thousand miles per
hour like fleas swarmed swarming the freshest
death sour
rotting from the inside out
diseased are you slowly but surely
the byproduct of this species filthy
or military as a shield
aluminum kevlar protecting
pretty soon making it impossible for
any spacecraft to leave
or even more so
for one to land
though as of now
the department of sanitation's route
unfortunately
does not include you so
more than curious
what are they going to do?

alien.

i have so much to say to you
the things
all of it
is to
all of you
the good ones
worse ones
the ones still figuring it out
but for now
somehow
i hope you'll find this book
and know
deep down
that if i come in anything at all
in love
i come
in peace

ufo.

my question is this;
unidentified by who?
unestablished by the establishment
unindicated by which?
unrecognizable by the one in question though
sightings saucers fly torched in sky date back as
far as we can remember and had a ways ancient
etch to stone pen it though still
undistinguished

all that matters
to me is
how you identify
not
how i identify you
or why even feel needed to

you are timeless in
not this.
not that.
beyond definition.

god.

all of it
in the stars
is you